UNLEASH YOUR GREATNESS

TRILOGY BOOK ONE

2nd Edition

The Journey: Catalyst to Change

Success is by CHOICE not by CHANCE. Find out your "what", be prepared for the "how" and embrace the effect of change "when" it happens.

Lovina B Akowuah

Copy Right© 2013 by Lovina B Akowuah

Publisher by LBA Consulting

ISBN 978-0-9897915-0-2

Unless Otherwise Noted, All Scripture Quotations Are
From The KJV Of The Bible.

Copyright © 1970 By Thomas Nelson, Inc.

Table of Contents

Dedication

I am dedicating this book to my dear children Afia, Kojo
and Jojo

Acknowledgments

First, I would like to thank God Almighty for his unwavering love, favor and blessings on my life.

I thank God for my children Afia, Kojo and Jojo. Their presence in my life has forced me to face my fears and learn to believe in myself so I could be a great role model to them. They are my rock and they have sacrificed a lot to make this journey possible.

To my husband Bernard aka "Big Head", who challenged me to greater heights, stood by me, and supported me every step of the way. He believed in me and has been a large part of my success.

To my parents, Esther and Hero Bhavnani, who not only provided me with the foundation on which I stand but also molded and motivated me into who I am today. I truly appreciate their belief in my abilities as well as their unconditional love and support.

To all the 5LINX Platinum Senior Vice Presidents who became my role models and proved to me that anyone could push themselves to greater heights.

To all my mentors especially Barry Donalson and C. Anthony Harris, who have filled me with knowledge and expanded my mindset to believe in the possibilities of life. Thank you, Barry for all your insight.

To Cecilia Oduro, Love Asare-Bediako and Vishnu Bhavnani for their editorial contributions.

To my business partners who challenged, inspired, believed in me and encouraged me to develop myself.

To all of my family who inspired me to start living in my greatness.

Reviews from Edition 1

Unleash Your Greatness is thought-provoking and powerful for all who must press their way through the crowds of hopelessness and despair. It will give you a new perspective when facing some of life's difficult challenges but propel you forward in spite of what others may initially think. The Author has captured the essence of her breakthrough journey by applying the Word of God, understanding Timing, and her Faith. This Book will assist you in the identification of key areas in your personal life that will help you transition into being all that God has called you to be. I have read it 3 times. Now, I'm ready for the next Book! ~ *Elder Deborah Hook*

The author did an outstanding job with this book, it seems as though she was talking to me. This is a must-read book and I would recommend it to everyone to pick up a copy and join us on the journey to unleash our greatness. What I got from this amazing book is that sometimes it's not the giant accomplishments that matter; what really matters are those little victories in our lives. Applying the compound effect is something that I am now adding into my daily life and it works. I also learned how to come out of my comfort zone and take action by faith despite the fear and discomfort that might come along the way, because there is no gain without pain. I can't wait to read book 2 and looking forward to continue with the trilogy of the "Unleash Your Greatness" series. Excellent Lovina, you are the best, stay blessed! ~ *Marie Fonfah –Conteh*

Success is inevitable for anyone who is looking for a great read or knows of someone that may need some motivation to catapult their business to the next level then "Unleash your Greatness" is the book for you! Each chapter gives you precise key points on what you should focus on during your journey of being an entrepreneur. Unleash your greatness is a guide book that's written in a manner useful for one who is a novice in their journey as a business owner or one who is well versed in business. I enjoyed it so much that I purchased a few copies to give to friends as a gift. I'm looking forward to the release of author Lovina Akowuah's second book ~ *Charnetta Watson-Laing*

Wow, this book is one of those books I will read over and over again. The author did great with sharing her life journey to successful entrepreneurship in a way which makes you reflect on your life journey. She helps you think outside the box and prepares you for creativity and positive changes leading to success. I love the quotations Lovina Akowuah uses in the book and can't wait to read the other two books to follow- Process of Transformation and Effect of Change. Personally, I'm very satisfied with the quality of the contents, very well written and will highly recommend to family, friends and any book club. Perfect!~ *Dazar Opoku*

I'm a success coach myself, and Unleash your Greatness by Ms Lovina made me feel so empowered. I'm actually using some of the material I got from this book to train and empower many people today. Great and unbelievable piece. Amazing for those who do not believe in themselves.~ *Lucie Matsouaka*

Once you pick this book up, you can't put it down. You are able to relate in so many areas. The Author shows you through her story how you can overcome obstacles and triumph to victory. This is a must-read from teenagers to adults!!! ~ *Maurice Clark*

This book is a very practical book. It draws deep on the reader to search within themselves for one good thing and perfect it! The author's relation to her own life experiences actually brought my attention to being perseverant, and come to think of it, that's what success is all about. She is able to clearly illustrate perseverance using her marathon event, which I think was awesome. You need to read this book to experience what the reader experienced. It is very capturing and motivating, and surely leaves you thirsty for more... Great book! ~ *Cecilia Oduro*

What a refreshing, inspirational, uplifting, motivational book!!!
I often read a lot of so called "self-help" books, so I definitely was looking for some new ideas. I found lots of new ideas and felt inspired throughout the entire book. It's an easy read and my attention was captured throughout. I'm so looking forward to the remaining books under this trilogy! ~ *Michelle Gray*

Unleash Your Greatness is a relatable book that inspires, informs and guides the reader to look within thim/herself to work towards their greatness. I would definitely recommend this book for anyone who feels like he/she wants more out of life. Can't wait to read the second book!!!! ~ *Abigail Sackey*

I used this book as a book club selection for a group of teenaged girls who were former DCFS state wards in my therapy Process Group. They absolutely LOVED the section on 'Characteristics of a Winning Attitude' and having the right mentor. It certainly hit home for this group of young ladies!

Lovina Akowuah gives a fresh, modern-day perspective on everyday challenges. I highly recommend this read for all ages and all walks of life! ~ *Angela Ratcliffe*

One of the things I liked the most about this book was that it was an easy read, but it was VERY impactful in its content. Mrs. Akowuah does a great job using her own very fascinating story to invoke a feeling of "I can change my life too" in the reader. I highly recommend this book for someone who is feeling like they are stuck in their career and anyone contemplating or just beginning their journey as an entrepreneur. CAN'T WAIT for the next book!! ~ *Gundi Simmons*

This book is an easy read but definitely engages a wide variety of readers of all ages. The author uses her own life experiences to help guide you in your quest to find the greatness in you. I could relate because the stories are not fiction, they are real life experiences that the majority go through. I urge you to read it because the author shares her experiences from where she began, and how she reached SUCCESS. She is definitely one of my role models. This is a must-read... *Sonia Tetteh*

Unleash Your Greatness has been a game changer and reality check for me! I always knew something was holding me back but this book gave me the right questions and perspective I needed to pin-point just what that something was. The book is simple to the point, yet insightful and thought provoking. I find myself frequently re-visiting passages and statements from the book and it has been a great check and balance system to getting me on the right track, and into high gear! Thank you Lovina Akowuah for being such a great writer and embarking on the journey of unleashing one's greatness! I am forever grateful for the tools and guidance you provided me! MUST GET THIS BOOK!! ~ *Nechelle Robinson*

Lovina's Book, "Unleash Your Greatness: The Journey: Catalyst to Change" is both inspiring and empowering!! It challenges you to search deep within yourself to find out what is really important to you ("Your Why"). It then builds on "Your Why" and uses it as a catalyst to push you to be your best self and do what it takes to realize and accomplish your dreams.

This book really helps you to take a deep look at yourself and understand who you really are, what you really want out of life and what is important to you. Once you understand who you really are, it is then and only then can you "Unleash Your Greatness" and be the person you were meant to be.

Thank you Lovina for such an empowering book! I look forward to book two!!! ~ *Lakeisha Howie*

Preface

Have you ever felt like you have been trampled upon your entire life? That nobody ever believed in your abilities, and that everyone just took advantage of your weaknesses and capitalized on them? Do you know you are unique and can unleash the greatness in you?

Unleash Your Greatness will take you through the life and journey of the author. It will unveil what motivated her and eventually became the catalyst to change her life (Book 1). She will also share with you the process of transformation; how she attacked her fears, faced adversity and endured all types of challenges while developing herself during the journey (Book 2). Book 3 will reflect how the effect of change exposed her to the inner greatness that she never knew existed inside of her.

Book 1: This book will focus on guiding the reader using the author's own life experiences to discover his or her catalyst to change how the reader can step out of his or her shell and walk the success journey for themselves. It will also prepare the reader for a successful journey as the author believes success is brutally challenging and most people need to be prepared to walk the journey in order not to surrender to failure. My mother used to quote Psalm 139:14 when I was very young.

*"I praise you because **I am fearfully and wonderfully made;** your works are wonderful."*

Although, I did not appreciate it at the time, I now do. With all I have achieved, I truly believe I am indeed fearfully and wonderfully made.

Do you believe everyone is made in the image of God and we are all born blessed? The universe is a very powerful force. As the saying goes, what you speak into existence will manifest into your life. I think a lot of people do not believe in that. I was very much inspired by my mentor, C Anthony Harris, whom I met four years ago. He is a firm believer in prophesying into your life, and he always made us stand up and say the following words:

SAY THIS OUT LOUD TO YOURSELF LIKE YOU MEAN IT

I Love Myself

I am the best of the best

I am beautiful

I am sexy

I am a winner

I am victorious

I am unstoppable

I am a champion

I am a winner

I will be successful

Repeat this to yourself every single day and watch the positive effect it will have in your life.

Introduction

My name is Lovina Bhavnani-Akowuah and I was born in Ghana, West of Africa on March 9, 1977, to my wonderful parents Hero and Esther Bhavnani. Being the second of four children, I had a normal childhood, grew up a very shy child and always lived in the shadows of my siblings. I obtained my elementary and high school education in Ghana, and moved to the United Kingdom in February of 1997 to pursue my college education. I enrolled at the University of East London and pursued a degree in Business Administration. Initially, I was confused as to my career path, but my father was immensely helpful in guiding me. Upon graduation, I worked as a Human Resource Analyst, while pursuing my master's degree in Business Administration (MBA). I subsequently moved to the United States of America in December of 2000 and being motivated by my strong ambition, almost immediately enrolled at Fairleigh Dickinson University in Teaneck, New Jersey, to continue my Master's program. I was still confused in life at this point and was not sure of what I wanted to major in. My first inclination in my ever-confused state was to major in finance, but that did not go well, as my interest in finance was not enough to motivate me. I then began considering Human Resource Management, possibly because of my prior work experience.

My pursuit of the "American dream" landed me a job with Computershare Inc., where I worked as a Client Service Associate for five years managing employee stock purchase plans and stock options. While still working, I completed an MBA in Human Resource Management. Upon graduation, I began my journey of frustration and struggle with Corporate America. At this point, I was almost certain that I had figured out the career path I wanted to take. However, after many months of fruitless job searching, I was completely broken. I had no luck finding a job in the human resource field. Unfortunately, I had to give up my new-found passion and dream. I thought things would fall into place automatically: go to school and the job should line up once you are done. But no! This was not true in my experience. While facing the pressures of life, feeling like a failure, thinking less of myself, I met the man of my dreams. I accepted a transfer to Illinois as a tax specialist and customer service associate, and subsequently relocated in

March of 2006. With that experience, I landed a position as a financial consultant with a leading insurance company.

Although this was a great job in and of itself, it remained just another job to me. There was no passion, no inner fulfillment and simply put, I hated my job. I kept soul searching and looking inside myself to figure out what my real passion was. I was lost in the shuffle, and realized helplessly that I always moved in the direction the pendulum swung. Every day, I found myself admiring my friends, who seemingly had found 'it', and even my husband Bernard, who had been able to identify his career path so easily and exhibited so much passion as an IT Auditor. The search for my passion was endless and extremely varied. I moved from wanting to own a daycare so I could take care of my children, to wanting to be a nurse, a financial auditor, a health care manager, you name it. I even started my own small-scale bakery called Vina's Tasty Pastries, with the hope of making it big someday. I had my plan mapped out and surprisingly doors were opened to my business. I was baking on weekends, early in the morning and late at night while still juggling a full-time job. I supplied to businesses, but expenses were high and I barely broke even to cover them. I enjoyed baking and even took classes to perfect it.

The one-woman shop was becoming tiring and very costly; costly to my health and family. With very little or no financial returns, I applied my business analysis skills I had learned in school and it led me to conclude that this was not a viable business; it was not worth the trouble.

I felt like a lost sheep. Each time I came up with the latest new idea, I would share it with my three wise "men" - my Mother, my best friend (Cecilia) and my husband. These people were my life support system. No matter how silly the idea was, they would nicely talk me out of it because I could never really elaborate on the plan. The reason was simple: I was not passionate about it. I was simply trying to find myself. I remember praying to God so many times and asking Him to give me divine direction.

Then, my first child happened. My daughter Afia was born in April of 2007. In November of 2009, my son Kojo was born. As if this was a rippling effect, in March of 2010, I found out I was expecting my third! At that point, I had a rude awakening: I knew I had to quit playing (although I never played, I just could not find myself), and get serious about what I wanted to do. I began intensifying my search and research for my career path. Work continued to be taxing and frustrating, coupled with no pay raises in four years and three little kids; I was miserable. Quitting my job was not an option at the time. My husband and I could not even afford to start a college fund for our second child, nor afford a proper daycare. We sought home care for my son, as early as when he was only three months old. What a cruel world it is, I thought. I often cried myself to sleep as I had always dreamed of giving my children what I had and more when I was growing up. I wanted to give them a life full of love, happiness and everything they needed to position themselves well in life. I was blessed to have parents who gave me the world. I completed my bachelor and master's degrees without any student loans which was a real blessing, but how could I do the same for my children?

I had to do something different. My first inclination was to go back to school and get a better paying job. But wait! I had done that already. I already had two business degrees which were wasting away! Why can't they allow me financial freedom, I asked myself. Why can't they allow me to give the world to my children?! I did a quick assessment of some of the people around me. My boss had worked for this company for more than 15 years, and he was still not the CEO. In fact a year prior, he had been demoted due to corporate restructuring and had just worked his way back to a managerial position AGAIN!! How could I get up the ladder? I had my doubts about it, but deep down, I knew it would happen one day. I just could not substantiate this feeling.

At the same time, America plunged into a deep recession: companies were engaging in mass layoffs or furloughing. Tension mounted both at home and at work. I would go in to work and wonder when I was going to get the tap on the shoulder followed by the pink slip. When my co-worker, who was clearly an outstanding employee, got laid off; I crumbled and continued to work in fear. Although I was fortunate never to have received the pink slip, I realized that there was no job security and things looked very unstable. The future of my job was very bleak. The storm was not over. As much as I tried to stay sane on the job, I was still given a bad performance review by my boss for reasons that were not clear to me. I felt I had been picked on because of my frequent maternity leaves. It got nasty when I tried to challenge his review, and of course, it yielded no positive results. Life at work was no longer the same. I gradually begun to ask myself probing questions as to why I needed to beg for a pay increase, when I knew I had earned it. And why I could not take charge of my life independently.

THE WHAT (Catalyst to Change)

"What" became the catalyst to change in my life? What was the one thing that opened my eyes to discover that there were bigger and better things a person could achieve? Have you always known you are not really living up to your full potential in life? Have you always known that what you are or may be doing today may not be what God intended for you to be or do? If you have had thoughts similar to these, you are probably right. I lived in that darkness for a long time until I discovered myself. Know that your situation should not be permanent. You have the ultimate control over your destiny and no matter what you do; things will not change unless you take action. If you had pushed yourself to the limit all the time, what would your life look like today?

Let's take a look at my journey. Ultimately, my journey should help you to reflect on your life and push you to search deep within yourself.

"SUCCESS IS BY CHOICE NOT BY CHANCE"

Once I found this quote and had a deeper understanding of it, it became a guiding force in my life. I knew then that as the saying goes: "You can lead a horse to the water but you can't make it drink" you ultimately have the power to control your destiny; nobody has the power to take that away UNLESS you let them.

Journal

Knowing yourself is really important. In order for you to look deep into yourself you really need to know and understand who you are. Up until now what have you thought of yourself? This reflection will be a starting point for you and for us along this journey when we start working on building belief in you.

What is your story? Take this page to write about
yourself…..

_____

_____

_____

_____

_____

_____

_____

_____

_____

_____

_____

_____

"Knowing yourself is the beginning of all wisdom." ~Aristotle

Up until now, how have you thought of yourself? What is your perception of yourself in terms of your achievements?

_____

_____

_____

_____

_____

_____

_____

_____

_____

_____

"Most people overestimate others' talents and underestimate their own." ~Orrin Woodward, *L.I.F.E. Living Intentionally For Excellence*

Let me prepare you for this and help you understand that you are unique in your own rights. You were made in God's image and you are fearfully and wonderfully made.

This is how I see you

You are the best of the best

You are beautiful

You are handsome

You are a winner

You are victorious

You are unstoppable

You are a champion

You will be successful

You are blessed

You are highly favored

∞ Chapter 1 ∞

Entrepreneurship and Why

Entrepreneurship is the ability for an individual to engage in a business venture for themself while managing all the risks that come with it to ensure profitability.

As a child, I remember being surrounded by many adults that I looked up to. Some were doctors, lawyers, teachers, engineers and business owners. They all made a good living and were well-positioned in society. I never thought about it, but the ones who were filthy rich and extremely successful were those who owned their own businesses. Most of them were not highly educated; however, they had become successful by choosing the path of entrepreneurship.

The society surrounding me promoted education to its peak, so it was only natural that you were expected to go to school and have a prestigious title that would reflect the status quo and make your family proud; but that involved working for somebody else.

In my years of education, everything I was taught talked about working in the corporate world. I was programmed that way. I was a naturally hard-working person. Everywhere I worked, I excelled and proved myself to be exceptional, but somehow corporate was not favorable to me. I was passed over for promotions numerous times when I knew I was more than qualified for the role and worse, the person who was usually awarded that position was someone I had trained. Although I was never given a valid reason why, my intuition led me to believe racism and sexism were in play. Then the economy took a dive and I realized I did not have any bargaining power to receive a pay raise, not to mention how I killed myself on the job and was not getting rewarded fairly. All these disadvantages were mounting up and I was starting to get really upset with my life and the path I was on. I started looking at different options that would allow me to feel free, have control and not put a glass ceiling on my success. That's when entrepreneurship knocked on my door.

Here are four main reasons why entrepreneurship seemed a more favorable option for me versus staying in corporate America.

Advantages of Entrepreneurship

Salary: Generally, people want to be paid for the amount of work they do in full; they do not want to be short-changed. Often people do not get compensated enough for the work they do and it makes them feel they are not being treated fairly. I considered myself to be an above-average employee and I put in my time; however; my pay increase was largely dependent on someone else's decision and that was not favorable to me. I was at a disadvantage for four years where my pay increase was almost nonexistent. When you work for someone else, you are at the mercy of his or her business decisions. If business is not doing so well, management could even choose to cut hours and paychecks. If you are the business owner however, you can take absolute control over your own paycheck. This was a reality check and a deciding point for me. I was so discouraged with my salary experience in the corporate world, it made perfect sense to put all efforts into my own business and control my income. The other deciding factor was the emergence of a suffering economy which led to so many people being laid off. Although I had never been a victim of layoff, I knew I was not immune to it either. The thought of not being so dependent on someone else and having control over my own fate was much more attractive than having the relative security of a regular paycheck.

Flexibility: Being an entrepreneur affords you flexibility. Having control over your work schedule means that you choose when to take time off and work the schedule that suits you best. God had blessed me with three beautiful children and so flexibility became very important in my life. Although the company I was with supported a family lifestyle, there were still so many instances where I needed to be with my children and I could not. I spent 10 hours a day away from my children and it felt terribly unpleasant. There were times when my children were sick and I still had to drop them off at daycare because my schedule did not permit me to be home with them. There were also many times when I had to work long hours and even on weekends to complete my workload without receiving commensurate compensation. If you had a workload it had to be completed, even if it seeped into your personal time.

One day when she was three, my daughter asked me a question that was so profound that it really got me thinking about my life. She asked, "Mummy, but why do mummies and daddies have to go to work? Do you know when you drop us off at daycare that we the little children, we cry?" Wow! What a mind-blowing question it was for a three year-old to ask me.

I knew then it was time to take charge of my life. Besides entrepreneurship, there was nothing else that I could think of that would allow me to have the flexibility I was looking for to raise my children. It would allow me to be there with them for class parties, games and a lot of other activities that made the children feel special. This was very important to me as I was raised by a stay-at-home mother and I knew that it made a world of difference in my life. I wanted to give the same to my children and not conform to what society expected us to do, which is to send our children to daycare.

<u>Decision-Making</u>: As an entrepreneur, you are able to make all the important decisions relating to your company. You have complete control. This provides a huge degree of independence and a chance to shape your own career as opposed to relying on decision-making from "above". Your idea of what could make a company successful may not be in line with that of the leadership, and this could cause a lack of autonomy and create dependency.

Owning your own business allows you to eliminate the hierarchy in decision-making, thereby helping decisions to be implemented faster and the results to come quicker. This was a huge benefit for me in becoming an entrepreneur because there were so many times I ended up working with people who had no interest in my career development and suppressed my growth as an employee. I was always at the mercy of a decision-maker as to whether my vacation days were approved or not, whether or not my pay increase request would be approved and whether or not I would get a promotion. In all these instances, I had to wait on someone to make a decision and the result of that decision could either advance or set back my career. As an entrepreneur I could pick and choose who I wanted to work with, and what direction I wanted to go on in my journey. If I wanted an increase in pay, I would simply work harder and reward myself with that increase. This sounded very fulfilling to me especially since I had experienced misery as a result of corporate decision-making.

Excitement: Entrepreneurship involves risk taking. Most business owners enjoy coming up with an idea and nurturing it to growth. They tend to love challenges and thrive on solving problems. Being an employee can really suppress your ability to think and nurture ideas because most of the time no one is looking for your opinion. You become a slave to systems and cannot provide input or solutions to a problem. I really enjoyed figuring solutions out, but I was never in a position where my solution was welcome and that made me feel like a follower, not a leader. I wanted to be part of the decision making and the problem solving. The adrenaline rush of actively working on a problem sounded very rewarding and the joy of solving the problem was one I looked forward to.

So with the decision made to venture into business ownership, the question became, what will I do? What will be the business venture that will allow me to blast off so I can end my days of being an employee? A lot of ideas came and left. Some were started and were dropped; however the one that stuck around was my introduction to direct marketing. The reason being everything about this industry gave me a great sense of fulfillment and it led me to discover myself.

Remember, everyone can choose a different path of entrepreneurship. You have to decide what makes you feel fulfilled and go for it!

Journal

Reflecting on your current journey is really important in us figuring out your "what"

What is your current profession.......

What are the great things about your current profession?

What are some of the not-so-great things about your current profession?

_____

_____

_____

_____

_____

_____

_____

_____

_____

_____

_____

"The only way to do great work is to love what you do. If you haven't found it yet, keep looking. Don't settle." ~ **Steve Jobs**

Are you feeling fulfilled? If not please write down why?

_____

_____

_____

_____

_____

_____

_____

_____

_____

_____

"A Fulfilling life is different to each person. You have to acknowledge your dreams, and not just wait for life to happen, and opportunities to come knocking at your door." ~ **Joan Lunden**

What have you always desired to do? What is it that you dream about all the time? What is it that you think you were destined to do? Think about this carefully and be specific.

_____

_____

_____

_____

_____

_____

_____

_____

_____

_____

_____

_____

_____

"Build your own dreams, or someone else will hire you to build theirs."
~ **Farrah Gray**

What has been holding you back from achieving your dream and heart's desire?

_____

_____

_____

_____

_____

_____

_____

_____

_____

_____

*"Walk away from anything or anyone who takes away from your joy. Life is too short to put up with fools." ~ **Unknown***

After completing this exercise, what comes into your mind about yourself. Write it down

I AM ....

Meditate on this Prayer

Lord, give me a vision for my life. I put my identity in you and my destiny in your hands. Show me if what I am doing now is what I am supposed to be doing, I want what you are building in my life to last for eternity. I know that all things work together for good to those who love you and are called according to your purpose (Romans 8:28). I pray that you would show me clearly what the gifts and talents are that you placed in me. Lead me in the way I should go as I grow in them. Enable me to use them according to your will and for your glory. ~ Stormie Omartian (A book of prayer)

∞ Chapter 2 ∞

The Making Of An Entrepreneur

My journey as an entrepreneur began in August of 2009, when my husband and I were introduced to an Inc. 500 company. This company used the direct marketing approach to offer its products and services. The company's goal was to recruit people to market its products and services by way of introducing others to the business using a direct marketing approach also known as "network marketing". It was my first time hearing this term and I kept wondering how this could possibly be profitable to me. Initially, the jargon and terminology got the best of me and the entire picture was blurry; but with time, I began to understand it.

I knew right away I had to be committed to learn and allow time to take its course. These are the steps I had to take to help me develop into an entrepreneur.

STEP 1:

Develop an Understanding:

Nobody was born an entrepreneur, so in order to develop a greater understanding of the journey you are about to engage in, it's imperative that you commit to learn and become a student of the path. Every business will have different nuances associated with it and the only way to learn is to dive right into it and embrace every experience. For example, if you are looking to start a bakery, you must take classes and learn everything you need to know to become the best pastry maker in your market, perhaps join a club, an association or maybe even attend meetings to network with the local bakery owners. No matter what kind of business you choose, you will need to take the initiative to understand the space you are moving into so that you can become an expert in your area.

That is exactly what I had to do. I had to enlighten myself to understand the whole industry. I did not want to become an average person. I made up my mind that if I felt so fulfilled to become an entrepreneur then I needed to excel in the industry I had chosen. With that said, I armed myself with information by ensuring that I attended all conference call trainings, regional in-person meetings and any national meetings that would help me to associate myself with the experts in the industry. This helped me to develop understanding and confidence in my area of choice. Some of the information which I learned about my industry is listed below.

Statistics showed that network marketing made more millionaires than all other industries combined. In 2012, network marketing and direct sales hit a new record of $167 billion in global sales [1]. Additionally, I learned about the direct marketing model and how it allowed you to earn money residually versus linearly. I also learned about how the system of direct marketing was similar to the model adopted by McDonald's, Wal-Mart and other successful franchises.

Once the concept of direct marketing became crystal clear in my mind, there was no turning back. This was it! God had finally opened my eyes to see. I am thankful that He did that sooner than later! He came through for me. This enlightenment and understanding helped me to develop and become an expert in what I did; without that knowledge I would not have survived.

TIP: Pick a path or choose an avenue that you would like to succeed in, and then achieve that dream by putting your mind to it.

STEP 2

Identify your areas of improvement:

I remember every time I went for job interviews in the past, the following questions were asked of me. "What are your strengths and what are your weaknesses?" I would like to assume you got asked that question too, right? Honestly speaking, most people have a ton of things to say about their strengths, but most people including myself always fail to tell the truth about their weaknesses for fear of not getting the job. We all know our weaknesses, but we tend to hide them and fail to face them. Facing your weakness is a very important learning curve on your journey as an entrepreneur your weakness may hinder your progress.

As I shared earlier, I had a very shy personality and still do for the most part; the direct marketing approach required me to face that fear. I asked myself how was I going to be able to convince people to believe in direct marketing when I could not even speak up for myself and kept a distance from assertiveness? I simply had to face a lot of my fears because I recognized that facing them would lead me to excel in the area I had chosen.

So, for you to move up and progress in your chosen path, you will need to reflect on yourself and identify the areas that you truly know will hinder your growth and progress and begin working on them. You have to ask yourself why some people excel at one thing more than others. It's simple; nothing will hold them back, not even their weaknesses.

TIP: The quicker you identify your weaknesses the sooner your learning will begin.

STEP 3

Express your Passion

Passion is key to survival on your journey as an entrepreneur. Without passion, your chances of marketing or selling anything to anyone will be very limited. Someone who has and expresses passion will get to the top faster than someone who does not. Remember, this was our first exposure to direct marketing and yet thankfully we were able to build a strong organization; in some instances faster than individuals who had been in this industry longer. Ninety percent of our success was attributed to passion. How do you develop passion? It comes from learning and understanding the path and journey you are taking. If you own a restaurant, your clients should feel your passion from your expressions and how you interact with them; it will help you get customers and keep them too. Nobody wants to buy from a grumpy person or from someone who cannot even express him or herself well about his or her chosen path. Without passion, you will be better of remaining an employee and living in unhappiness

My passion came out every time I spoke and presented my business opportunity, to the point that people bought into me first before the actual opportunity they were being presented with. When you have the chance to interact with someone, in most cases you have just one chance to create a good impression and at that moment you need to shine. If you truly believe in what you are doing, it needs to show and people need to feel your commitment and excitement. Lack of passion can also knock you out of the game faster than anything else.

TIP: Believing in your service, product or opportunity will draw others to believe in it too.

STEP 4

Learn from your mistakes

Mistakes do happen and they happen for a reason. Without mistakes, learning will not take place and without learning success will be difficult to attain. A lot of people fail to learn from their mistakes, and continue to repeat them over and over again until they let their frustrations knock them out of their journey to success. They hold on to their frustrations too long and cannot let go. They most likely conclude that it just did not work for them. I cannot even begin to tell you all the mistakes I made in my learning and development process. However, I made a commitment to myself that each time something went wrong, I needed to figure out the right way to do it so I could teach it to someone else.

The business model of direct marketing requires you to develop and help your team. Your team's success is an integral part of your success, thereby creating an environment that fosters selflessness and sacrificial help. If I learned and developed myself, I could shorten the learning curve for others and help my team grow and expand faster.

Learning from your mistakes is necessary in any journey that you take as it promotes personal development and growth and enhances your ability to coach others too. As the saying goes, experience is the best teacher.

TIP: If you have not made mistakes, you lack experience.

STEP 5

Ask for help and help others

You need to recognize that someone has been there before you, and has invested time to learn the business. The individual faced a lot of hurdles and has learned from them. You have to understand that people will not assume you need help unless you reach out for it. You will be surprised how much information you can get out of someone by simply asking for help. You will realize, 'Wow, had I not spoken to them, I would have made a huge mistake or invested in something wrong'. When an individual begins any journey, there is a lot of excitement and enthusiasm and this causes him or her to do a lot without being strategic. Failure to ask for help could firstly lead you to make more mistakes than necessary and usually waste a lot of time.

I have always been a person who is never shy to say, "Please show me how". In many cases, you might have to ask for help from someone who is looking up to you in certain areas that you don't have strength in. That is very tough for a lot of people for fear that their employee, mentee or in direct marketing terms "down line" will see them as lacking knowledge.

I also realized early that in order to become truly successful you have to be ready to be a servant to others as well and by default, your blessings will follow. As I mentioned earlier, one of the reasons I chose to pursue human resources was to be a corporate trainer, as I enjoyed sharing my knowledge with people. I found this business to be an opportunity to train people on how to develop their financial abilities and turn them into successes. With my enlightenment on how direct marketing worked, it was clear that all I had to do was to pass on my knowledge and by default, I could leverage everyone's success, not just mine.

Robert Kiyosaki, in his book "The Business of the 21st Century" explained that in order for an individual to move from the employee side of the cash flow equation to the investor side, he has to learn to have money and people work for him rather than he work for money and other people. I thought this was phenomenal! In a nutshell, network marketing would help me to develop myself and other people, as well as help me develop the mindset and new skills needed to grow and be a success story. This is exactly what I needed.

STEP 6

Allow Time

Many people don't have the patience to wait for their breakthrough. They are looking to build success very quickly and therefore don't have the patience. They expect to breakeven right away but do not understand that most traditional businesses take five to ten years to reach a point where they are in full gear and making lots of profit. I concluded that, if the system does exactly what I wanted it to do for me, I need to sacrifice 5-7 years perfecting this model, then I could save myself from working for somebody else for the next 35-40 years and have enough money to retire on. I am not a financial guru, but I am very comfortable with numbers and facts. The numbers were clear and the facts were undeniable. All I had to do was to stay focused, be determined and be a go-getter. What the mind conceives, the body can achieve.

In the beginning, we still weren't fully comfortable with it, at least not to the extent of quitting our jobs and investing ourselves full time. Like any regular American family, we had tons of bills to pay, and two children to take care of; it was important that we maintained our status quo, as we could not afford to take a risk and fail. I say this because most people quit their jobs too soon when they begin the journey of entrepreneurship, but we knew we had to be strategic about it and make the right moves at the right time. The immediate step was allowing me to come home first and eventually with time that is what we did.

TIP: Everything can happen to everyone if only they allow time.

In spite of all these steps I undertook to begin and become an extraordinary entrepreneur, I understood very quickly that it was not going to be easy because as per a Multi-Level

Marketing statistics in 2012 [2],, for every 100 people that took this path, less than 1% were successful. I wanted to be a part of the 1%. You can also find the success rate in your chosen path to help you understand what you are up against.

I was so determined and hungry for financial freedom, I could taste it at the tip of my tongue. With much determination, I started "THE JOURNEY". It was not meant to be a get-rich-quick scheme, but a journey that was going to boost my children's financial future. This was a journey that would allow me to give the world to my parents and my entire family, a journey that would quite simply change my life forever and help me to impact society positively, a journey that today has allowed me to develop and uncover my true potential. This potential was not obvious when I was a regular employee. It was hidden and remained in its pristine form for such a long time that it would have completely gone to waste, had I not taken this journey.

In "The Business of the 21st Century", Kiyosaki states "Network Marketing is a great personal development kind of business. It is about building them up so that they can take better control of their life. It allows individuals to grow and realize their full potential in life." **And that is exactly what happened to me.**

Journal

Developing an understanding of your "what" will help you to confirm the path you are looking to undertake

Write down again what you wish to accomplish and become…

_____

_____

_____

_____

_____

_____

_____

_____

_____

_____

_____

_____

"Nobody ever wrote down a plan to be broke, fat, lazy, or stupid. Those things are what happen when you don't have a plan." ~ **Larry Winget**

On a scale of 1 to 10 how knowledgeable are you about this choice? ....

On a scale of 1 to 10 how passionate are you about this choice? ....

Do you have all the skills you need to succeed on this path? Yes or No.................

If not, are you willing to do whatever if takes to accomplish this desire? ....

Based on the previous questions please identify what you need to work on in general. For example: developing knowledge. This could be multiple things.

List down each step/task you need to accomplish for your dreams to come to reality and write down your estimated date of completion.

Task   Date of Accomplishment

_____

_____

_____

_____

_____

_____

_____

_____

_____

_____

_____

"Small victories ... It's not about the big wins. It never has been and never will be. It's about the small victories in life that make the next day, moment, meeting, gathering etc. doable. Everyone needs the small victories to keep them going - to give them hope. Everyone!" ~
William James

You are ready to begin. There are some dream stealers in your life. Who are they? Write down their names

_____

_____

_____

_____

_____

_____

_____

_____

_____

_____

_____

Beware of dream stealers, they are everywhere and they come in different forms so be alert ~**Lovina Akowuah**

What steps are you willing to take to change your circle of influence?

_____

_____

_____

_____

_____

_____

_____

_____

_____

_____

You are the sum of the five people you are surrounded by so if you don't like who you are, you need to change your circle of influence ~
Lovina Akowuah

After completing this Exercise, what comes into your mind about yourself? Write it down

I AM ....

Meditate on this Prayer

Lord, I know your plan for me existed before I knew you, and you will bring it to pass. Help me to walk worthy of the calling with which {I am} called (Ephesians 4:1). I know there is an appointed plan for me, and I have a destiny that will now be fulfilled. Help me to live my life with a sense of purpose and understanding of the calling you have given me. Take away any discouragement I may feel and replace it with joyful anticipation of what you are going to do through me. Use me as your instrument to make a positive difference in the lives of those you have placed in my path ~ Stormie Omartian (A book of prayer)

∞ Chapter 3 ∞

Questions and Activities for

Reflection

So let's talk about YOU. There are several methods that can help **YOU** to discover yourself. In my situation, it just so happened to be the discovery of entrepreneurship through direct marketing. I encourage you to find that vehicle and commit to it. My goal is to help you reflect deeply on yourself and unleash the greatness you have in you through the finding of your "WHAT". When you find the "thing" that brings out the best in you, that "thing" becomes the catalyst to change in your life. Commit to it, because commitment is the greatest requirement. No matter what happens, allow yourself to be pushed to greater heights.

So the question is: How do you know that you have found your "Thing" or your "What"?

The thing that will serve as a **catalyst to change in your life**

Here are some obvious characteristics of how you will know when you find it

It should give you the inner satisfaction and self-fulfillment that you desire in life.

It should challenge you to face your fears.

It should push you to develop yourself and become a better person.

It should keep you awake at night.

It should cause you to break some habits.

It should push you to question your choices in life.

It should cause you to make some sacrifices.

So earlier on I asked you to write down the one thing you dream about. Does it fit all these characteristics?

Founder and publishing editor of success magazine Darren Hardy and author of "The Compound Effect" once said there was power in writing. So I urge you to write and envision what you write. What you are thinking is merely a fantasy until you write it down. Take the first step to write it down! Writing makes it a reality.

When I put this into practice, the benefits of inking down my goals were far more rewarding than I had ever imagined. It provides a vision, and that vision will manifest in your life as you see the notes you have written down every day. Try it, it works!

"You can't cross the sea merely by standing and staring at the water."
~ Rabindranath Tagore

Activity

So maybe you have felt that you are not good enough to achieve the goals you wrote down earlier. You have bottled up all the feelings in you and have never really expressed them to anyone.

This is the chance for you to write down all your deep feelings, your disappointments, the people who hurt you and made you feel this way (write their names). The intent is to pour it out and let the emotions GO!!!

❖ _____

❖ _____

❖ _____

❖ _____

❖ _____

❖ _____

Life is filled with disappointments, anger, pain and more. We all have people in our lives who have hurt us and disappointed us. Imagine that you are walking with a sack over your shoulder and the sack is filled with rocks. Each rock represents a person who has hurt you. It is going to get very difficult for you to keep walking with those rocks. If you let go, the weight will be lifted and there will be no burden on you. You will now have the clarity and the strength to climb your ladder of success. Writing it down will help you to finally deal with the pain and forgive those who have hurt you.

"Don't let today's disappointments cast a shadow on tomorrow's dreams." ~Unknown

Now that you have let out your feelings, I want you to understand that I felt the same way. There are many people out there just like you and me.

Who are those negative people in your life that hold you back and do not encourage you to discover yourself? Write their names down. At this stage, you will need to figure out how to surround yourself with like-minded individuals who will be a positive impact in your life, for example, members of your church.

You have people in your life who do not encourage you and always hold you back, yet it seems very difficult to pull yourself away from them. Every time you try they suck you right back in. The question is, do you want to keep living a life of misery or do you want to break free of your surroundings so you can achieve better things in life? Follow your heart and be strong. If you surround yourself with people who care about you and want to see you succeed, eventually you will be able to completely break away from those negative people. You can do it!!

"You cannot expect to live a positive life if you hang out with negative people." ~Joel Osteen

Now that you have identified what you want to do in life, released your pains and identified the negative people, it is now time for you to envision your success. Envisioning your success is key. You need to believe in yourself and start speaking into your life about your success. The power of "I AM"…. Will slowly erase all of the years of negative words that have suppressed you your whole life.

When you affirm "I AM" statements daily, your soul becomes totally identified with the truth of that statement at the very depths of consciousness where all human perceptions cease to influence the outcome and where all creation originates.

Here are some affirm actions to start you off with your belief.

AFFIRM-ACTIONS

I AM A WINNER

I AM A CHAMPION

I AM THE BEST OF THE BEST

I AM UNSTOPPABLE

I AM BEAUTIFUL

I AM STRONG

I AM BEAUTIFUL

I AM SUCCESSFUL

I AM VICTORIOUS

I AM AMAZING

I AM DEBT FREE

When I was working in the corporate world, one of the things that helped me get through my work day and complete all my goals for the week, month, and quarter was to create a to-do list. I relied on it so much because it helped me to visualize my journey to completion. It gave me a great sense of accomplishment when I checked off a task and helped me to envision the end result. It worked like a charm!! I believe that if we all practice this on our journey, we will be able to celebrate the small victories.

"Small victories ... It's not about the big wins. It never has been and never will be. It's about the small victories in life that make the next day, moment, meeting, gathering etc. doable. Everyone needs the small victories to keep them going - to give them hope. Everyone!" ~ *William James*

We are on the right path if you continue writing your goals down and speaking your dreams into existence.

I AM ....

(FILL IN THE BLANKS)

I AM ....

(FILL IN THE BLANKS)

I AM ....

(FILL IN THE BLANKS)

I WILL BE ....

(WRITE DOWN YOUR DESIRE)

Remember, you are FEARFULY and WONDEFULLY MADE Psalm 139: 14

"14 I will praise thee; for I am fearfully and wonderfully made: marvellous are thy works; and that my soul knoweth right well."

∞ Chapter 4 ∞

5 Key Guided Principles

I would like to prepare you for this journey. The journey may not necessarily be smooth sailing, but it is important for you to understand that life is not meant to be smooth. Those who push through the excruciating pain are those who finish successfully. So before we proceed, let me ask one more time.

Are you SICK AND TIRED of the life you are living?

Do you WISH for change?

Are you READY to unleash your greatness?

Jim Rohn from his audio book, "*Building your Network Marketing Business*" indicated that the same wind blows on all of us, the wind of disaster, the wind of opportunity , the wind of change, the wind of upside and downside and more. Everyone has a different arrival. For some it could be one year, for others it may be two or three years, but what matters is that you keep moving in the same direction, and make the second year better than the first, and the third year better than the second. To borrow my Mom's favorite saying, "It is not the beginning that matters; it is the end that matters most." The keyword is for you to **WISH** for change. It is never too late for anyone. I am here to tell you that you can make the next few years better than the last several years if only you WISH to. To do that, you simply need to implement some key disciplines and principles in your life to ensure that change arrives for YOU.

My goal, after you have read this chapter, will be to help you shorten your learning curve and help you achieve your goals faster, by sharing certain principles which took me four years to discover. Just remember that these principles helped me through my journey, and if utilized well, should help you through your journey as well. Please make a mental note of the fact that this will not be an overnight process. Change is necessary for you to move to the next level in your life and it is important that you embrace and prepare your mind towards the journey. At every stage, just remember how you are doing this journey and why.

A renowned speaker, Art Williams, delivered a speech to the 1987 National Religious Broadcast called the "Just do it Speech". This speech has become a classic philosophy of winning in business and life. His speech focuses on how many people procrastinate in life.

TIP: Whatever you desire in life, this is your chance, "JUST DO IT".

Art Williams mentioned in his speech that "The primary difference between winners and quitters is that, the winners do it and do it and do it and do it until the job gets done and they spend more time talking about how they did it and how they did not quit like everyone else."

My favorite quote: *"Quitters never win and winners never quit."*

A winner is someone who, even though he or she has hardships in daily life, does not get discouraged to the point of giving up, and perseveres to attain his or her goals.

A quitter is a person who quits or gives up easily, especially in the face of some difficulty, danger, roadblocks or more.

So are you going to be WINNER or a QUITTER? If you want to be a WINNER, "JUST DO IT".

4.1   The Compound Effect

I really hope you are not beginning this journey thinking that you will be looking for success in 30, 60 or 90 days for that matter. I hope you are not planning to give up after a 90-day period if you have not seen success. Bring out the winner in you and keep trying until you see success. It does not end there. Once you succeed, you have to maintain your life in success mode. This I would call sustainability. This advice is priceless! It was a lesson I learned the hard way, as I had spent years looking for instant results in everything that I did. Let me use my weight loss challenge as an illustration. I would do a crash course and lose 20 pounds, staying off carbohydrates but it was not sustainable; which is a very important tool to use on your journey. I felt not so healthy and was always frustrated. The key was the sustainability part. Even in my business, I remember many times when I would want someone to make a decision right away to partner with me, a negative response would completely destroy my day and/or week. In my personal life, I remember too many times when my whole family would complain about me being impatient and craving for an audience. It was like karma, when I had my daughter, the apple did not fall too far from the tree. I realized that I had done myself a major injustice by just not being patient. I had an eye opening moment when my mentor Darren Hardy introduced the "Compound Effect" to me through his book; "The Compound Effect (Multiplying your success, one step at a time)". He likened it to a light switch that had just been turned on in my brain. Wow! What a discovery it was! If only I had known about the Compound Effect a decade or two ago, life would have been so different, and I would have saved myself a lot of heartache.

So what is the Compound Effect? The Compound Effect is a series of tiny steps taken consistently over time to gradually make a drastic change. It is the only process you need for ultimate success on your journey. So in other words, if you make small smart choices in life and ensure that you do it consistently, over a period of time, a radical change emerges. Most of the time, society expects us to do massive things to show the payoff and so a lot of people tend to give up on their dreams too soon when they do not see instant results. Success is rarely instant, well except for the lottery. Even in the lottery situation, it is rare to buy tickets the first time and win. You usually would have been buying the tickets for a while.

When we started our network marketing business, our friends made fun of us, as they expected to see an instant massive change in our lifestyle. They watched like hogs and talked behind our backs. Despite the lack of support around us, we pressed on. In the first year of starting the business, we made some money, but it was not very significant. In year two, business was starting to mature, and in year three, we started to experience significant changes. It was then that our success had begun. We had started taking family vacations, our personalities changed, and even our attitude towards life changed. Of course, we had not become snobs, but had just started to experience the value of money and how it could greatly impact a lifestyle. In year four, they were done laughing and now moved to admiration from a distance ... So the question is: What if I gave up after year one because there was no massive change in my life and caved in to people's ridicules? What if? I would have given up on the ripple effect of what consistency and time would do in my life.

Let's look at another example. How many of us have tried losing weight year after year by cutting down dramatically and then given up 30 days after spending weeks eating a salad, because we still do not notice any change in our waist line? Or even worked out every day for a month and did not see any change? We are all guilty of this, right? In hindsight, if I had made a consistent change by ensuring that I did not eat after 7 p.m., committed to a healthy breakfast and lunch, and worked out consistently 3-4 times a week, the change would have been long lasting.

The secret is that things take time to unfold in life and anything that is easy to come by is easy to go. True lasting success requires work and lots of it. Giving up before the blessings and permanent change arrive means ultimate failure. In my opinion, it is worse for you to start and not finish, than to not start at all.

Take for instance a couple that can only afford to save just a dollar a day. A dollar a day in a year yields $365 and over a 10-year period, it would multiply to $3,650. This is a typical example of the Compound Effect. The couple took baby steps, but after 10 years, they could boast of comparatively significant savings. Doesn't it feel good when we do very little and ultimately enjoy success?

So what if you begin your journey and people are watching and you try and you fail, and you try again and you fail? Do you believe you need to try again or you need to walk away from it?

A good friend of mine took the nursing board exam 12 times and failed, over and over and over again until she passed on the 13th time.

How about a foreign qualified doctor who migrated to the United States and passed her board examinations to do residency after her fifth try or the chartered accountant who just could not qualify and ended up being nicknamed the "King of Accounting?" What if that was you? Would you have walked away after the third time? What if any of these people had quit? They would never have become the nurse, doctor or accountant. It boils down to how determined you are to succeed and to achieve that dream you have always had.

See the Compound Effect is a principle that you need to use to guide you because of its predictability and measurability. It prepares you to understand that you do not need to take huge steps to achieve your desire, but to simply take little consistent steps. By using this method, you will reach your goal. It's not a race! It is more about endurance. Remember: Slow and steady wins! Who said there was a certain speed ratio to achieve success?

4.2   Mindset

Having a Positive Mental Attitude (PMA) at all times is very essential on this journey. Without an unstoppable positive mindset, all hope of surviving this journey will be short-lived.

So let's look at some characteristics of a winning attitude.

Characteristics of a Winning Attitude

Powerful 'WHY': You have to make sure it is boldly written down. Earlier on we identified what your WHY is and I had you write it down. It is important that you reflect on your WHY everyday because it is very easy for you to forget why you are embarking on a journey when your WHY is not at the forefront of your mind. Secondly, your WHY has to mean a lot to you, to the extent that the very thought of it makes you very emotional. This should give you the energy to be perseverant. Finally, your WHY needs to be bigger than you. It is very easy for us to give up on ourselves, however if your WHY is about somebody else, your chances of entertaining defeat will be minimized to almost zero.

BELIEF: Belief is another characteristic of building your mindset. What is belief? It is a state or habit of mind in which trust or confidence is placed in some person or thing.

"When you believe in something and you carry it in your heart, you accept no excuses, only results" ~Ken Blanchard

"By believing, one sees" ~ Emory Miller

You need to establish BELIEF in yourself. So when we reflected on your life, we wrote down all your fears, disappointments, pain, negativity and more. All of these have suppressed your confidence, am I right? Remember these are thoughts and feelings that have been recurring throughout your whole life and you have subconsciously allowed them to take over your life. But we are going to tackle that by working on your conscious mindset. Once again, it begins with affirmations, or in this case what I call "affirm-actions".

SAY THIS OUT LOUD TO YOURSELF LIKE YOU MEAN IT

I Love Myself

I am the best of the best

I am beautiful/ handsome

I am sexy

I am a winner

I am victorious

I am unstoppable

I am a champion

I am a winner

I will be successful

Repeat this to yourself every single day and watch the positive effect it will have on your life.

Since these negative thoughts have consumed you for the better part of your life, it is important you recognize that building this mindset is not going to be an overnight transformation, but rather a work in progress. The principle of the Compound Effect will reflect on this path too.

- Don't let someone tell you that you are not good enough. Believe in yourself.

- Don't let someone tell you that you will not make it on your journey to achieve your heart's desire. Again, believe in yourself.

- Know that you are more than what someone else is saying you are WORTH.

You also need to establish belief in the path that you have chosen to take. Remember, when you went through the thought process of deciding the journey and finding your "what". You made the decision based on the fact that it gives you inner satisfaction and self-fulfillment, and it keeps you awake at night, right? So if that feeling continues to exist within you, why let someone else steal that dream away from you? During my struggles in the beginning of my entrepreneurship journey, I asked myself one question: Why should someone else cause you to think that their hustle is better than your hustle, when there are different hustles measured at different degrees and under different circumstances?

Robert Kiyosaki in his book "The Business of the 21st Century" wrote "We live in a cruel world, if you are poor they step on you, if you are not successful they step on you, if you don't have confidence, they step on you, so it is up to you to gain the confidence, the skill set, the mindset, the guts, the determination to not care what other people say about you". This became a guiding force on my journey and continues to strengthen me as an entrepreneur and also in the process of developing that unstoppable mindset that we all need for success.

Create a Winning Environment: In order to develop this unstoppable mindset, you need to create a winning environment that supports, sustains and nourishes success. Your environment must match your ambitions. It is time for you to stop taking advice from those who have not reached any heights in their life because they are likely not to have any great advice for you. Make it a must to surround yourself with people who are always supporting you to reach higher heights and not people who drag you down. The saying goes that you are a sum total of the five people you are surrounded by. So look around you and if those five people you are mostly surrounded by are not successful, then you need to surround yourself with doers, movers, shakers and high income earners who will show you a thing or two about how to become successful.

Invest in yourself: The first success tip I learned as an entrepreneur when I was developing my positive mental attitude was that, those who invest in themselves will realize success faster than those who do not. When we are cheap on ourselves, we get cheap results. You must feed your mind by investing in educational tools such as tapes, books, training events and more. Again, remember that the mindset development is a process. Imagine for a second that you stop listening to your favorite radio station in the car and replace it with a motivational audio CD which you listen to over and over again. It starts to erase all the unconscious negative feelings and thoughts that have filled you and over time, your conscious mind will remind you that those things were never true anyway. So I encourage you to take time to invest in yourself because it will be much more rewarding than using that money at a social event with the friends who are not looking for change and will not serve as a positive influence in your life.

While you are building this unstoppable mindset, understand that challenges will still be inevitable. The highway to success is a toll road. You will still encounter some negative people and dream stealers, you will face some rejections, and you will experience some failures.

Perseverance: Another characteristic of having a winning mindset is perseverance. What is perseverance? It is a continued effort to do or achieve something despite difficulties, failure, or opposition. It is being resilient, no matter what.

"I've missed more than 9,000 shots in my career. I've lost almost 300 games. 26 times, I've been trusted to take the game winning shot and missed. I've failed over and over and over again in my life. And that is why I succeed. ~ Michael Jordan

Ultimately it will boil down to your WHY. Remind yourself everyday of what that WHY is and use that to push yourself up the ladder.

Another famous quote I want to share to prepare you for this Journey:

"The road to success is not straight. There is a curb called Failure, a loop called Confusion; speed bumps called Friends; red lights called Enemies; caution lights called Family. You will have flats called Jobs. But, if you have a spare called Determination; an engine called

Perseverance; insurance called Faith, and a driver called Jesus, you will make it to a place called Success!!"

I share these quotes with you to help you understand that these roadblocks are not channeled specifically to you, but channeled to everyone who desires to achieve success in life. Those who push through these roadblocks are those who succeed and finish well in life, period!! There is no other way around success but for you to fully embrace these challenges and persevere through them. Most often when we look at successful people, we only see the end result of their success but never get to see what goes on behind the curtain. Anyone who has succeeded and gone through a journey to unleash his or her greatness has had to develop an unstoppable mindset and was willing to endure all the pain that came on his or her journey. That's what I am preparing you for.

Focus: Focus is also a characteristic of having a winning mindset. I encourage you to focus. Focus stands for (F) follow (O) one (C) course (U) until (S) successful. Most people start one thing and in a few months drop it and move on to the next "hot" item. Does that sound familiar?

"Consider the postage stamp: Its usefulness consists in the ability to stick to one thing till it gets there." ~ *Josh Billings*

"One reason so few of us achieve what we truly want is that we never direct our focus; we never concentrate our power. Most people dabble their way through life, never deciding to master anything in particular. ~ *Tony Robbins*

The decision you made about your "what" was not just something that passed through your mind. You chose it because it is something you have always dreamed about. It keeps you awake at night and it gives you self-fulfillment. If all these facts remain in your mind, then I urge you to stay focused and keep pushing. Success is right here and it will come to you if you reach out for it. God has given you the ability and you are going to succeed.

Enthusiasm: The last characteristic of a winning mindset is enthusiasm. Enthusiasm is having great excitement for or interest in a subject or cause. If you have passion for your goals and desires, others will too. Often times, people would ask me how I was able to build success in my direct marketing business. My response: Passion! I was always passionate every time I spoke about my business and noticed that I transferred this passion to others. Most people chose to partner with me to do business, not because of the information I shared with them, or that I was charismatic, but because of my enthusiasm and passion for the business. Enthusiasm is magnetic and it draws people to you.

"Enthusiasm releases the drive to carry you over obstacles and adds significance to all you do." ~ Norman Vincent Peale

Again, if your "what" gives you inner satisfaction and self-fulfillment, expressing enthusiasm about it should be fairly simple to do. If you are passionate about something and that passion bursts out of you readily, the chances of someone stealing that dream away from you will be very minimal.

I hope by now you are in full understanding of what a powerful mindset can do for you in achieving your goals. I am confident that if you practice every single day and you do something little every day in building this unstoppable mindset, there will never be anything in life that you cannot achieve; because once the mind expands, it can never shrink back and the sky will be your limit.

4.3   Choices and Habits

At this point, we know that success is not going to come in ninety days, and we know that we have to work on our minds to strengthen us through this journey. The next thing to do is to make the right choice and break or develop habits that will sustain us through the journey. Notice that I keep saying journey, right? Everything is a process and has to work hand in hand over a period of time for long-lasting success.

Choice is an act of selecting or making a decision when faced with two or more possibilities. Choices are at the root of every result. Each choice starts a behavioral pattern. Choices can be our best friend or worst enemy. At some point in our lives, we have had to make a decision. Once you hit the crossroads, whether you choose to be happy or sad, go to college or not, be successful or unsuccessful is all your decision to make.

"You are 100% responsible for what you do, don't do or how you respond to what happens to you."~ Darren Hardy

When I began my journey as an entrepreneur, I was so excited about sharing the solution to financial problems with all my family and friends. That was simply a bad idea.

TIP: NEVER INVOLVE FAMILY at the early stages of your business, especially if you love them, you MUST separate business and family in order to maintain a continued relationship with them.

My hunger for direct marketing disgusted some of my family members; it was so bad that I refrained from talking about my business. I was monitored when I was in the midst of "their" friends to ensure that I was not talking about my business. To them, I was ridiculing myself. My husband and I became the talk of the family and still are today, despite the success we created for ourselves. Friends looked at us as "weird" but after a while when our mindset started to develop, we shook it off. Always remember: What does not break you will only make you stronger. It simply gave us the strength to work even harder, because if I gave up on myself then I would cave in to their ridicule. My relationship with my family was strained and often I asked myself if it was worth losing my family and friends because of the path I had chosen. The positive part about all of this was I had the support of my husband. We were in this together and that made a world of difference. How different was my business from opening, for example, a restaurant by a family member or friend, especially when both would yield profit? The ultimate goal for both would be financial freedom. So why then should I allow myself to be a laughing stock? Direct marketing taught me SHORT TERM SACRIFICES FOR LONG TERM GAIN. Meaning you will need to give up a lot of things you are used to doing such as watching TV, shorten your sleep time by waking up an hour early and going to sleep an hour late.

The fact is that most people are complacent in life and cannot comprehend why they have to hustle. Most people would prefer not to hustle, but rather work for someone else for forty years and then go work as a greeter at Wal-Mart or Home Depot when they retire, because they never chose to do something different. The question is why do 95% of people who choose to be complacent in life feel they have the ammunition to ridicule the 5% that have chosen to be different? It was simply not fair. But is life meant to be fair?

I was at the crossroads and had to make a <u>CHOICE</u>. If I listened to my critics, it would mean I was giving up "MY

DREAMS" for the world, and I was NOT prepared to do that. I had to brace myself and continue climbing the ladder. I knew that once I made it to the top, victory would prevail and it would be worth the ridicule.

So I had to make a choice every time there was a conflict between a family gathering and a business meeting. My business meeting always prevailed. I missed a lot of parties, and lost a lot of friends. I also became distant with some family members and the only reason was: I had to FOCUS. These were really hard choices, but it was necessary for me to disassociate myself from the negativity so I could stay focused. I also made a lot of sacrifices along the way and these sacrifices have paid off a lot in my life today.

To you, I say this: In order for you to move up, you have to be prepared to make a lot of difficult choices; choices that you are not used to making, but are essential for moving to the next level.

"It's not hard to decide what you want your life to be about. What's hard is figuring out what you're willing to give up in order to do the things you really care about." ~Shauna Niequist

"It does not take much strength to do things, but it requires a great deal of strength to decide what to do." ~ Elbert Hubbard

Some choices will be difficult, but life is all about making choices and good choices at that! Always do your best to make the right choices and if you happen to make the wrong choice, do well to learn from it and move on.

Up until now, you have probably made some poor choices in your life. It could be that you chose to buy a pair of new shoes instead of investing that money, or you chose to associate yourself with friends who are not motivating you or you keep eating unhealthy foods and you continue to gain weight. The point is all those choices have not allowed you to develop and progress, so why continue that path? Why not build the mindset of making the right choices this time around so that you can achieve different results?

Ultimately, your life is a reflection of the choices you make. If you do not like the life you're living, it is time to start making better choices.

So, take a second and pause every time you have to make a decision before you do anything drastic and you will be amazed at how things will move along in your life. It's time for all of us to wake up and make empowering choices. Wake up and smell the coffee!

Habits: A habit is a recurrent, often unconscious pattern of behavior that is acquired through frequent repetition or an established disposition of the mind or character. A habit is hard to give up.

"A daily routine built on good habits is the difference that separates the most successful people from everyone else" ~ Darren Hardy

Often times we come across people who are extremely good at what they do to the extent they are admirable. I learned that these individuals were so good because they had cultivated a habit of perfecting their craft through practice. Michael Jordan is a very good example of someone who practiced many free throws. When he was interviewed he said, *"I am not out there sweating for three hours every day just to find out what it feels like to sweat."*

When I started my business, because of my zest to perfect my understanding of my business, I spent a lot of time learning everything about my virtual office. I knew everything about what everyone was doing in my organization. I was glued to my computer and I checked and double checked everything. A lot of my business partners would ask how I could remember everything, and I simply said I studied my virtual office. This positive habit that I cultivated brought so much success in my business and helped me on my journey. I also spent a lot of time practicing my presentation and learning everything. I would play back pre-recorded presentations over and over again until I perfected them. I was far from being a public speaker, as I was a very shy person. So good habits cultivated over a period of time through practice can be very rewarding in our lives and bad habits cultivated over a period of time can be very detrimental to our lives. No one can tell you what those bad habits are. Author Stephen King once said, *"A man who can't bear to share his habits is a man who needs to quit them."* This is a simple way for you to identify those bad habits in your life and quit them.

Most of us have learned certain habits unconsciously without knowing it. We all have to be aware of what those bad habits are, so that we can consciously work on getting rid of them. There are times when I get into this mood of eating non-stop for a couple of weeks. I say to myself, "Well, I haven't gained any weight", but before I know it, this bad habit will compound and suddenly a rush of 10 pounds will befall me." What I am trying to say is: We may think our bad habits are very insignificant and therefore should not be an issue, but when compounded over a period of time, they cause a lot of strain in our lives.

Today I encourage you to sit back and identify those bad habits that you need to get rid of so you can get out on your own to invite success into your life, because ultimately success is not looking for you, you have to go and find it.

Please take a moment to write down some habits you know are not helping you in your life and work towards changing them in the next 21 days.

4.4   Have the right Mentor

A mentor is a person who guides a less experienced person by building trust and modeling positive behaviors. An effective mentor understands that his or her role is to be dependable, engaged, authentic, and tuned into the needs of the mentee.

TIP: Everyone needs a mentor. Even the mentor needs a mentor.

I believe that if you find the right mentor in life, your journey will be well structured and you will not have to spend too much time reinventing the wheel. The key is finding the right mentor.

I believe that a person can have a distant mentor and an upfront and close mentor. When I started my journey as an entrepreneur, I had a lot of role models whom I wanted to emulate; I watched and observed them from a distance, meaning, they were my distant mentors without their knowing. I simply made sure I followed their trainings and would be present whenever there was an opportunity to learn from them. There were also people I could call, on and others I could speak directly with to ask questions and get their opinions. Those were my upfront mentors. A mentor is a person you have to carefully pick in your life. So how do you know the difference between a good mentor and a not-so-good mentor?

According to John Maxwell's book "Mentoring 101", *"A mentor shouldn't be someone who would like to make themselves better at the expense of someone else, rather a truly successful person or mentor would like to raise others up and they don't feel threatened by the thoughts of others becoming more successful than them. Raising you others should be a successful person's joy and not threat."*

Most people feel that a mentor has to have some special skills, but mentors are regular people who have the qualities of a good role model.

Here are some characteristics of a good mentor according to a research paper done by a UCLA graduate division. [3]

Mentors listen

Mentors guide

Mentors are practical

Mentors Educate

Mentors provide Insight

Mentors are accessible

Mentors criticize constructively

Mentors are supportive

Mentors care

Mentors succeed

Mentors are admirable

One mentor during my time whose name keeps coming up even after his death is Jim Rohn. He was known as one of America's foremost philosopher who shared his success philosophies and principles for 46 years until his death in December 2009. He coached and mentored many people and one of the people who succeeded him is Darren Hardy, who propounded the theory of the Compound Effect.

Growing up, I felt a great sense of satisfaction every time I shared knowledge and impacted someone with information that helped him or her progress. During my process of discovering my "what," I considered becoming a corporate trainer. The industry of direct marketing placed me in a position to train, mentor and coach others. This gave me an inner satisfaction and sense of fulfillment. Someday I truly hope, I will be a great mentor to many just like all of my mentors, especially Barry Donaldson and C Anthony Harris who throughout my four-year journey as an entrepreneur have embodied all of these characteristics I share with you today. I am so lucky that I can call on them for advice, guidance and learn from them. They are so selfless and quite frankly have invested a lot of time in grooming a lot of individuals to be successful like them, and they do it with love and care.

"People will forget what you said. People will forget what you did. But people will never forget how you make them feel." ~Bonnie Jean Wasmund

Everyone needs a mentor, someone to keep him or her on track to attain his or her ultimate goals. I urge you to find that mentor who will embody most if not all of these characteristics; ensure that you stay close to them for guidance, support, and knowledge. A person without a mentor is always going to walk in circles in the dark, until they ask for direction. Just think about it this way: If you put an address in a global positioning system (GPS) to go to a certain destination, it is possible that the GPS will take you in the wrong direction. Then you stop to ask for directions from someone who you feel is familiar with the area. Once you get back your sense of direction, you re-calibrate and keep going. This applies to our life and our journey to success. You need direction and a mentor who will serve as direction in your life.

My mentor Darren Hardy and I

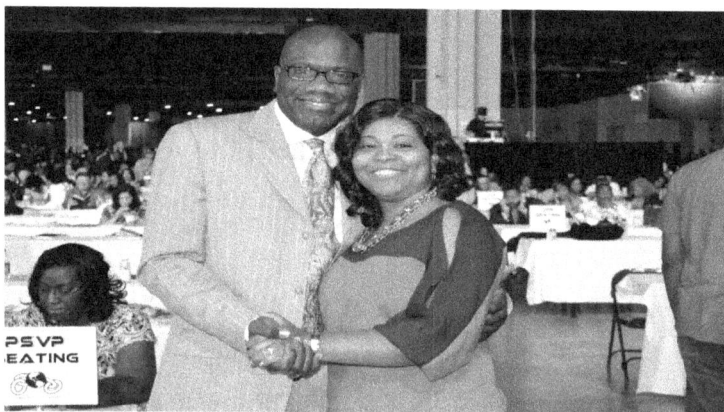

My mentor Barry Donalson and I

4.5   Develop the Faith

Don't worry, I am by no means a minister and I am not about to preach to you. I am only going to share with you my journey and how faith has played a part in it. Your faith can be in any religion. Whatever that religion is, it ultimately will play a role on your success journey. My religion is Christianity, so this section is Christian-based from a Christian's point of view.

How many of you know it is very easy for you to get off course with your God? We all know he is the ultimate and we cannot achieve everything in life unless we submit everything to him right? Well, it is easier said than done because it happened to me.

I have always been a follower of Christ and will always be a follower of Christ. I was raised in a Christian home, went to church every Sunday and have a mother who is a fervent follower of Christ; she is very prayerful in all aspects. I know I continue to live today because she has interceded on my behalf many times and she continues to do so.

Life got in the way for me when I became an entrepreneur. In the beginning, I was so focused on success that I started slacking in my prayer and walk with the Lord. I started missing church because I was traveling and that was my excuse. "No worries", I said, "God understands, I will just pray and read my Bible". Then praying started to diminish. Of course, I did not notice that the lack of prayer had any impact on my life because I was really doing big things. Success was coming and I was so engulfed in it. God has a funny sense of humor; He will just sit back and watch you till you fall flat on your face. So as the journey went on, little did I realize that with success come enemies. I was not planted in the Word and because of this, the enemies started really attacking me. One day I was talking with a very good friend of mine and she gave me a powerful insight; she said,

"God is never going to necessarily open the doors for the enemy to come in, but because you are not planted He will not hold them back from coming." Well, usually you think you know it all until it is said to you in a different light and that was an eye-opener for me.

The word of the Lord says: *"Be strong in the Lord, and in the power of His might. Put on the whole armor of God, that you may be able to stand against the wiles of the devil."* ~ *Ephesians 6:10-11 (NKJV)*

He also says in his word to those who follow him that: *"No weapon formed against you shall prosper, And every tongue which rises against you in judgment you shall condemn. This is the heritage of the servants of the LORD, and their righteousness is from Me, Says the LORD"* ~ *Isaiah 54:17 (NKJV)*

These are my two favorite quotes. Darren Hardy could not have said it any better in his book, "The Compound Effect". People are either motivated by what they want or what they do not want. A person can hate you because you have achieved something they have always wanted to achieve and/or because they do not have it in them to achieve what you have achieved. That could cause them to despise you and hate you. I know I am right because I live it. The fact is, sometimes it is necessary for us to have those enemies or haters in our lives because they give us a reason to fight. For example, David had Goliath to fight.

Enemies give us a reason to sharpen our skills and persevere to achieve our goals because without them we lose our strength and our purpose. Although they are necessary, I also believe you need to pray against them because whether we like it or not **Ephesians 6:12-13 says**: *"For our struggle is not against flesh and blood, but against the rulers, against the authorities, against the powers of the dark world and against the spiritual forces of evil in the heavenly realms. Therefore put on the full armor of God, so that when the day of the evil comes, you may be able to stand your ground, and after you have done everything, to stand."(NIV)*

As I shared with you in the beginning, my goal is to ensure that I share with you some guided principles I have used so that YOUR journey to success will be shortened.

Once I had a full understanding of what to expect in my life and journey, I knew I had to arm myself and I continue to do so. My favorite daily verse and prayer is Psalm 35.

"Contend, O Lord, with those who contend with me; fight against those who fight against me. Take up shield and armor; arise and come to my aid. Brandish spear and javelin against those who pursue me."

I encourage you to pick up the bible and read this verse every single day. Read it out loud, say it like you mean it and watch how you become surrounded by the Holy Spirit.

TIP: Getting planted in the Lord is essential in any walk or journey you decide to take in life period!

Journal

Preparing your mind is necessary for your journey

At this point you have identified your "what"

You have identified the steps needed to ultimately accomplish that task

We need to strengthen your mind in order to begin the process

To prepare you we need to identify your WHY.

Your WHY should answer the question, "Who is looking up to you and what is the reason you cannot fail at your goals? The answer has to make you want to cry and it has to be bigger than you. What is your WHY?

_____

_____

_____

_____

_____

_____

_____

_____

_____

_____

_____

_____

"He who has a why to live can bear almost any how."~**Friedrich Nietzsche**

You need to give yourself a realistic timeframe to commit to your "what"

Please don't write 90 days. It should at minimum be over 12 months. For Example, I decided to commit 3-5 years in the beginning of my journey.

_____

_____

_____

_____

_____

_____

_____

_____

_____

_____

*"If you make the unconditional commitment to reach your most important goals, if the strength of your decision is sufficient, you will find the way and the power to achieve your goals." –***Robe Conklin***

Besides your "what", what is the one thing you have always wanted to do that seemed unattainable?

The goal is to apply the compound effect to complete that goal. For example I used that to run the marathon. This in turn empowered me. Read the compound effect chapter and apply to attain a minor goal.

_____

_____

_____

_____

_____

_____

_____

_____

"Small victories … It's not about the big wins. It never has been and never will be. It's about the small victories in life that make the next day, moment, meeting, gathering etc. doable. Everyone needs the small victories to keep them going - to give them hope. Everyone!" ~ William James

What are some not so good habits that you know you need to work on. Please list them down. The intent is for you to take the next 21 days to change them as most habits are formed in 21 days.

_____

_____

_____

_____

_____

_____

_____

_____

_____

_____

*A change in bad habits leads to a change in life.~**Jenny Craig***

You have to make some choices that will help better your life and help you to accomplish your goals

Write down some better choices you are willing to make to help yourself to grow and get closer to your goals

There are two primary choices in life: to accept conditions as they exist, or accept the responsibility for changing them. ~**Denis Waitley**

List down a few people you know and want to emulate in your chosen path. The goal is for you to start surrounding yourself with them and learn from them.

_____

_____

_____

_____

_____

_____

_____

_____

_____

Your environment must match your ambitions

~ *Lovina Akowuah*

Select a mentor/mentors and ask them to mentor you.
When you do, you have to be prepared to listen and follow
their lead. Refer to Chapter 4 Unleash your greatness to
understand the Characteristics of a right mentor

Write down their names and why you chose them

_____

_____

_____

_____

_____

_____

_____

_____

_____

_____

Everyone needs a mentor. Even a mentor needs a mentor

~ ***Lovina Akowuah***

Let's reflect back on your "What"

Does it have the following Characteristics?

Will it give you the inner satisfaction and self-fulfillment that you desire in life

Will it challenge you to face your fears?

Will it push you to develop yourself and become a better person?

Will it keep you awake at night?

Will it cause you to break some habits?

Will it push you to question your choices in life?

Will it cause you to make some sacrifices?

If the answer is yes, then we are ready to begin

YOUR AFFIRM-ACTIONS

I AM ....

I AM ....

I AM ....

I AM ....

I AM ....

I AM ....

I AM ....

I AM ....

I AM ....

I AM ....

You will write this down and stick it on the wall for your daily routine of speaking positive into your life.

∞ Chapter 5 ∞

Running the Race

This chapter will take you through how I was able to incorporate some, if not all of these principles I have shared with you earlier into running my first half marathon.

I am not a runner and have never thought of myself as one. Growing up, I struggled with my weight a lot. I was always on some sort of diet, always jogged and walked briskly here and there; but it was mainly for weight loss purposes. For some reason, I started talking about my desire to run a marathon in 2006. The desire came to me and each time I procrastinated and always had an excuse for not participating. You get the picture? Can you relate to passing goals from one year to the next. It wasn't until my mentor Darren Hardy said to me: "A goal is merely a fantasy unless you have it <u>written down</u>". In January of 2013, I wrote down on my goal list for 2013.

- **Run a Women's 5K**   **June 2013**

- **Run the Chicago Half Marathon**   **September 2013**

I looked at it every day. At that time, it looked very bleak. I had written it down and pasted it on my wall and everyone saw it. I was forced to be motivated towards it. Because of this, I could not turn back.

Back in 2006 when I had that burning desire to run the marathon, I never thought about doing the half marathon. I only thought about the full marathon of 26 miles and that seemed difficult to achieve. It was not until the Compound Effect got introduced into my life that I realized that, well I can build upon it by starting with the half marathon which was 13.1 miles. So the plan was for me to run the 5K and build upon it to run the 13.1 miles. And I also decided that since this was my first marathon I was not planning to be a superhero. I was okay just finishing the race with a run/walk combination. See in the past I was so concerned that I had to prove my macho powers by running the whole course but again, the enlightenment of the Compound Effect helped me understand that in life you can do things at your own pace. The important thing is finishing the race.

So I registered for the 5K and before I knew it, June was here. I ended up not running the 5K because eventually that date coincided with a training program that I really needed. Normally, a person would have given up and said, "Well, I missed the first goal, so oh well." But I was determined, because as the saying goes, it's not how many times you fall but it is how many times you get back up and move on. I started asking and researching running groups and could not find any. That was indeed a roadblock and there were times I felt like giving up, but the fact that I had it written down made me push on. So the training began on my own. Some days I ran and some days I didn't. In the middle of the summer, it took me an entire month to get back to my running schedule, and there were just eight weeks until the race. Finally, I walked into a sports shop one day to pick up new running shoes and I happened to meet a personal trainer who led a running group. Wow, I had found yet another mentor! I so needed a mentor at that point as I was so lost and had no clue what I was doing.

It was eight weeks to my race. Was I too late to build up stamina for the race or could I still succeed? I remember a few weeks prior, I had met an old friend who was a runner and happened to be running the same race. When I told him that the longest run I had ran so far was two miles, he chuckled at me in a way that meant, "Girl, you need to forget this because you can't make it."

I said to him, "I am going to run the race and I will finish it." This is an example of an affirmation I had to make to myself every day.

Lucky for me, I found the **right coach.** He embodied everything a mentor should be. He told me he believed in me, he would help me and he knew I could do it. Exactly, what I needed to hear. He put together an eight-week training program for me. When I saw the training program, I was shocked. I needed to train for a 13-mile race. He put me on a program that required me to do two days of short runs, one day of a long run, two days of 30-minute workouts and two days of rest. That was how my seven-day week was designed. But the irony about the short runs was that it was very short. Forty five minutes of running for two minutes and then walking for three. I had to do the same routine on my long run. The minute I saw the program I thought to myself, does this guy know what he is doing? I need to build for longer runs. Is he joking? I would never finish the race at this rate. I picked up the phone and questioned the program (professionally, of course) and he said "TRUST ME, Lovina! I know what I am doing, follow this schedule and the rest will follow."

Here is the reality of what he was doing for me. The principle of the Compound Effect was being applied in my training program and I had not realized it. I only saw it after the first week of my training. But the lesson here is: I sought out a coach and he was going to take me through this journey. The running group alone allowed me to be in an award-winning environment. This environment allowed all of us to share our fears, our failures and our success stories. This alone was what I needed as everyone in my current circle was not running a marathon, so no one could advise me nor share in my thoughts and feelings. Additionally, I received weekly inspirational emails from my coach. I knew I had done the right thing to invest in myself in this training program

Starting the Journey is Easy

Just like anything else, starting the program was easy, I had a lot of energy and I was ready to make this desire come to fruition. I followed the training program he had designed for me because my experience as an entrepreneur had thought me to be coachable and to follow a system. If the system was not broken, there was no need to change it. I finished the longest distance I have ever done in my life during my first week of training and I was so happy and guess what? I didn't pass out.

Many of us start a journey with determination and enthusiasm; as long as that determination exists we will continue to achieve things we never conceived possible.

"What distinguishes those of us at the starting line from those of us on the couch is what we learn through running to take what the days give us, what our body will allow us, and what our will can tolerate." -John Bingham, running writer and speaker

The above quotation applies to all aspects of life and the journey we take to accomplish a goal. The biggest step is starting the race and maintaining the enthusiasm by learning from the experience.

Complacency can set in:

My training continued with ease, but along the journey I realized that when I derailed from my training program it had a ripple effect on my results. But I did not let those get to me. My second week came with a lot of distractions, however I stayed focused on my goals and ultimately accomplished my end of week goal for week two. The lesson I learned from my second week's experience was that I let my first week's success consume me I lacked humility. Because of that, I found it a little more challenging to accomplish my goal. This situation is very typical of a lot of people who are working on achieving their goals. The minute they have a victory, they forget about the journey and start celebrating too much and that usually causes them to lose their focus.

With that said, week two was very challenging. I had to give it everything I had. I was in excruciating pain, but I persevered. I had to realize what many people would give to have the simple gift of staying focused, achieving a goal. I did not need to take the experience and the opportunity for granted.

There are many people out there just like you who have dreams and desires, but starting the race alone is a challenge. It is a great accomplishment just to begin the race for your success. The first step is to identify that desire and goal; thankfully you have already accomplished that during our reflection process.

Distractions are inevitable:

As I continued my eight-week journey, I was faced with an even greater distraction along the way. It just so happened that we had a nine-day vacation planned ahead and so I was about to face some real challenges and distractions. I stayed focused on my goals. I made sure I followed through with my training despite being in an unfamiliar state and environment. That week I was not able to accomplish everything but I had programmed my mindset. I had developed the unstoppable mindset of not quitting no matter what failures I was faced with. Failures will come many times in any path you choose or any journey. How you handle the failures will determine the end result. My experience as an entrepreneur had exposed me and taught me that the more you move up the more challenges there are. Those challenges and failures will shape you as well as shape your journey. I don't believe there is a single successful entrepreneur out there who has had a smooth sailing journey to the top, confirming that distractions are common and inevitable.

The importance of having a mentor:

As if my coach knew I was in need of some motivation, he sent me a video of a father, Dick Hoyt and his son Rick, who compete together in marathons and triathlons across the country. Rick is physically disabled and as a father-and-son team, they strive to help those who are physically disabled become active members of society. The video was entitled "YES U CAN". Please go to *www.teamhoyt.com* to check it out for yourself. I sat in my chair and cried like a baby. I watched this video before my long run that Saturday. Had I not watched it, I may not have completed my goal. This is what having a coach can do for you; therefore it confirms the need for a mentor and most importantly surrounding yourself with like-minded individuals to motivate and inspire you. When you are faced with adversities, they will be there to guide you through the pain.

During my vacation, so much happened; I incorporated all the tips my coach had shared with me but despite all that I considered myself a failure. I was inconsistent for almost two weeks but I knew I just had to shake it off and move on. I reported my experience to my coach and he said something to me that was so profound. He said, "Lovina, please remember we are not looking for perfection, we are simply looking for consistency." He quoted to me again the principle of the Compound Effect. I was not supposed to be perfect; I just needed to stay the course. I needed to shake it off and move to the next week with confidence and determination.

"I always loved running ... it was something you could do by yourself, and under your own power. You could go in any direction, fast or slow as you wanted, fighting the wind if you felt like it, seeking out new sights just on the strength of your feet and the courage of your lungs." - *Jesse Owens*

The one thing that we all need to realize is that everyone will have a different journey in life. The great thing is, you are the only one who controls the pace that you want to go. You can move very fast and break some records or you can move slowly based on what you can tolerate. As long as you stay the course, you are still further ahead than the person who never started. Many people have desires, plans, ideas and goals; but they are never able to even start trying to achieve them. That makes you a very special person and a winner. However, because of the turbulence in the path that you have taken, you will need to understand that there will come a time when you will lose steam and the guiding force of a mentor will help you to finish the race.

Push yourself to the Limits:

As time went on, my goals increased. These goals were meant to push me to greater heights. If you are looking to achieve something in life, you cannot maintain the same pace. You have to increase your pace and push yourself to get one step further than the previous time; that is exactly what I experienced during my training. At this point, I had trained myself to run 8 miles as I had missed the opportunity to train for 9 miles because of the distractions I faced. This particular week, my goal was to finish 10 miles. I was so tired by the eighth mile because that was the level my body had been trained to endure. Most people give up when they reach their comfort zone or satiation point. They refuse to stretch themselves any further. Your success will require you to become very uncomfortable. It will require you to stretch yourself beyond your satiation point and that is exactly what I had to do. I had to brace myself and modify my routine. Sometimes in life when the journey gets tough, that's when we need to muster up the courage we have in us to finish the race. Those who push through the pain are those who finish well in life.

On that day as I was going through my mental struggle of finishing the course, I looked to my left and saw an older lady who was fully geared up and brisk walking with ease. I said to myself, if she can do it then I need to push even harder. Oh, the joy I felt when I finished my 10 miles! I was excited and I felt a huge sense of accomplishment. As the journey gets tougher in life, you will need to ensure you are surrounded with the right kind of people and have the right mentor in your life. Understand that, the only reason I was able to get the inspiration to finish my 10 miles was because I was in an environment where a lot of people were training to finish their race and someone's energy served as the last push I needed to finish my race. If we translate this to our lives and the goals that we all have, it will help all of us to understand that you should never be alone. If you want to become a Barber, you need to associate yourself with barbers all the time. If you want to open up your own bakery, you will need to network and learn from others who are doing it already. I hope you get the picture.

Becoming obedient to the process:

After my success story in regards to finishing my first-ever 10-mile run, it took me three days for my body to heal. I was in so much pain. In spite of that, I was so determined to do better. I contacted my mentor and sought his expertise. I realized that he had reduced my weekly goals going into the finishing part and I wondered why he would reduce my miles getting closer to the race. He gladly explained about the "taper period". The taper period is the time from 21 days away from your race to the day of the race where you run less and rest more; the rest is what will make you stronger on the day of the race.

Although this was not relatable to entrepreneurship, I was obedient because he was the expert in this field. He also explained to me that if I was able to run 10 miles by myself, then I would not have any trouble finishing 13.1 miles with thousands of other people surrounding me.

A lot of times when we are on a journey, we tend to feel that we have a little bit of experience under our belt and we start becoming disobedient to the experts because we feel like we know. Unfortunately there will always be a detour that you may not foresee, which your mentor will know about because he or she has already traveled that path. We have to be humble enough to receive guidance to ensure that our journey is shortened and ends well; after all experience is always the best teacher.

I say this because even though I listened and agreed with his expertise, I also derailed from my coach's advice slightly and of course that had a negative effect on me.

TIP: Never take shortcuts in life. Stay the full course. Change is permanent, sustainable and not temporary.

Adversities will show up again:

As if the race day was not enough of a challenge, things started happening to me from every angle. I dropped a five-pound weight on my right toe. To make matters worse, I chose a rough running path a week prior and was feeling terrible pains in my right knee and left shin. It was so painful that I was not able to train well during that week. By Saturday the pain was so bad that I was not able to complete my long run at all. This caused a lot of anxiety for me. I was not sure of myself anymore. I cried my way home and immediately contacted my mentor. He asked me to take things slow and to believe in the seven weeks of training I had accomplished. I started ice therapy on my legs, but it didn't seem to have any effect. I started hearing the negative voices in my head. I was afraid of what might happen as I had worked so hard to accomplish this goal.

"The voice in your head that says you can't do this is a LIAR."

The pain continued. I was instructed to do light running by my mentor. I added hot therapy daily, morning and night. By the end of the week, it seemed to be getting a lot better. My mentor did not let me strain it with practice for fear of injuring the knee further, so I only did light workouts just to get my body to remember the process. It was painful and I was a little worried, but I stayed focused.

"It's easier to go down a hill than up it, but the view is much better at the top." -Henry Ward Beecher

I was not going to let this stop me from getting what was mine. I trusted that my experience would pull me through because I was not prepared to let the devil have control over me. People are always watching and rooting for your failure "Yes, that's right Your failure!" Don't ever think people are happy for you to achieve greater heights better than they. The ones who laugh with you are the ones who are praying and hoping for you to not succeed because you will be one step ahead of them. For that reason, your critics alone should give you the determination you need to get through your adversities as they are necessary for you to appreciate your end result. With this experience, you can also serve as a role model or a mentor to someone else. So embrace the experience and learn from it.

RACE DAY (SEPTEMBER 8th 2013)

This was the moment I had prepared for. We got to the race site at 5:30 a.m. for a 7 a.m. starting. I had already accomplished and fulfilled my first fear by being at the start line. I texted my mentor and thanked him for his support. Without him, I would not even be there. The race began and it took everything in me to mentally believe in the training program I had used and practiced with for the last 8 weeks. We planned that I would start by increasing my run time in the beginning. If my knee bothered me too much, I would reduce it. In the past, I would usually worry about what others would think if I started walking after some time. But the unstoppable mindset and the belief that I had built strengthened me to get past that. It seemed my first mile would never come, then my second, third, fourth and fifth. By mile five I thought to myself, "This is much harder than my training". Just when I started having fears and doubts, I heard someone screaming my name.

"Lovina! I am here, you are doing so well. Keep pushing!" Guess who it was: My coach! Wow, just when I needed that extra push, he was there! What an incredible person he was. I had definitely chosen the right mentor. He was my rock! I kept pushing at mile nine because I had missed the required pace. I had come too far to give up. The problem is most people give up in life too quickly.

TIP: Life is not a race. It doesn't matter how fast you cross the finish line. It matters only if you cross the finish line.

I was focused and kept running then my cell phone battery died, which meant I had no music motivation. It was all mettle at that point. At mile twelve, my coach appeared again, calling, "Lovina, you are almost done. This is it. Just go and get your finishers medal!" This was it for me. I was ready to cross over. This was the day I had worked hard for, this was the day I could achieve something that I previously never thought possible.

Till today, I am not sure what would have become of me, had I not heard his voice and the motivation he gave me. It took very little for him to inspire me. I just needed to hear someone tell me I could do it. We all need that on our success journey. We need to hear that little positive voice as we go along this path because it is not easy at all. This confirmed to me that we all possess the ability to accomplish anything we set our mind to because God has built us that way. Your mind is what will ultimately push you to finish the journey.

I also never knew this, but along the 13 mile course there were motivational quotations everywhere, they were meant for you to read, but either way it was all to strengthen your "MIND".

The principle of the Compound Effect had made it possible, having the right mentorship had made it possible, being surrounded with the right people and environment had made it possible, having the right mental attitude had made it possible and finally faith had made it possible.

The moment of crossing the finish line was one I had dreamed about and envisioned. It was fulfilling. I HAD DONE IT. I DID IT, I DID IT, I DID IT! HURRAY!! What a blessing, what an accomplishment and what an Experience! After the finish, my mentor told me how many people passed out close to the finish line and I considered myself blessed! How close are you to your finish line? Are you considering passing out and giving up? Why not give yourself that extra push to get over the hump? Do you still think you can do this by yourself without a mentor?

These are all questions I pose to you to help you reflect on your journey. Success is yours. It can only be achieved if you take the right steps.

As you can see from my eight-week experience I have shared with you, the journey was not smooth. I didn't have to be perfect, it mattered most that I stayed the course and followed through. I had a lot of distractions and challenges, but it mattered that I picked myself up and moved on. I was not supposed to be perfect; I simply had to be consistent. I did not maintain my 13-minute pace, but it mattered that I crossed the finish line. Who cares about how long it takes you to cross the finish line, or the imperfections along your journey? Who are you looking to please, Yourself or others?

Make a decision and stick with it. Understanding that whichever path you choose will require commitment, dedication and willpower to cross over the finish line.

Me at the FINISH LINE!

Conclusion

Growing up, like many of you, success was talked about a lot. I heard it all the time. However, I never knew how success could be attained. My environment was centered on education and becoming a professional; pretty stringent, right? Well that's what I thought too. My environment was about having a higher achievement motive. Most of us have been put in that bubble. Expectations from our environment were high and forced us down a path we never desired. Your true feelings of what gives you self-fulfillment has diminished and have been suppressed over a period of time; because you felt you could not speak about them or voice them out to anyone for fear of embarrassment or shame. Am I right?

This was the bubble I lived in until August of 2009 when I was introduced to direct marketing and the world of entrepreneurship. Before that, I was told to go to school and get a good-paying job and that is how society deemed us as successful. However in 2009, my concept of success changed, my mindset was enhanced and I had a whole new understanding of what success can be for a person.

I heard this all the time when I was growing up and never really understood it until now. "A job is not a job if you truly enjoy what you do." So I ask you this: Is your job just your job or is it really not a job because you are living what you desire to do? I was miserable on my job and that's how I knew I was at the wrong place. I cried all the time and my poor hubby had to hear me cry all the time. I HATED my job with a passion. I felt so unfulfilled with the path I had taken. There was no question or doubt in my mind about which one I wanted to keep and which one I wanted to lose when direct marketing was introduced to me.

You don't have to be stuck in this bubble. If you are miserable, why continue to conform to society and what others want for you? Why live a life of misery? Who do you want to be remembered as when your Maker calls on you? Society is becoming more dynamic. We need to allow the future generation to live its greatness. But how can you guide them if you are not living YOUR greatness?

Ultimately, my goal after you have finished reading this book is to have helped you to understand that life can be what you want it to be. You have greatness in you that is probably latent and remains in its pristine form. You still have the chance to discover that greatness. Understand that you have conformed all these years, so breaking out of it will be a challenge and there will be a lot of resistance from society. But as I shared throughout the book, you have to take what is yours and make it work for you; understanding that you are creating a legacy for the future generation but most importantly living your desires and your dreams.

Let my story and my journey motivate and inspire you so you can also unleash the greatness you have inside.

Good Luck in your Journey!!

You are the best of the best

You are beautiful/ handsome

You are a winner

You are victorious

You are unstoppable

You are a champion

You are a winner

You will be successful

Psalm 139: 14

*"I praise you because **I am fearfully and wonderfully made**; your works are wonderful"*

Unleash your Greatness. is a "trilogy": a series of three books

Book Two will focus on the "How". It will share a comprehensive transformation process experienced by the author while guiding the reader through his or her journey. The journey to success is brutally challenging, and the obstacles faced by most can cause them to "QUIT". Book Two will ensure the reader understands the nuances involved in the journey to success and strengthen the reader to overcome those obstacles when faced with them; understanding that it will be a transformation process.

"Challenges are what make life interesting and overcoming them is what makes life meaningful." ~ Joshua J. Marine

Book Three will focus on the "when". The effect of change once you have gone through the transformation and how the effect will ultimately open your eyes and lead you to discover and unleash your greatness. Most people are unsure about their true purpose in life until they go through a transformation process.

"Man cannot discover new oceans unless he has the courage to lose sight of the shore." -Andre Gide

Take this Journey with me and let me help you…..

About the Author

Lovina Bhavnani-Akowuah, MBA, is a woman of faith, a dedicated mother, wife and entrepreneur. Her love for helping and coaching others began more than ten years ago while she was searching for a fulfilling career path. Since then, she has built a huge network of entrepreneurs who are seeking financial success. She's also coached thousands of individuals to develop a strong mental and emotional attitude. Today, she continues to mentor, inspire and motivate others through her own struggles, challenges and accomplishments.

Lovina believes that the journey to greatness is brutally challenging, however most people are uninformed and are usually unprepared when faced with any struggle, challenge, distraction or adversity.

It is a result of these struggles and challenges that prompted Lovina to author "Unleash your Greatness". This is a "trilogy": A series of three books; that will take the reader through the journey of the "what" (Catalyst to Change), the "how" (Process of Transformation) and the "when" (Effect of Change). She believes that with the right mentor and coaching, a person can have a rewarding journey to success; if they have the desire to win and are prepared to overcome their challenges! She focuses on coaching individuals to unleash their greatness.

Lovina was born in Ghana West Africa, studied in the United Kingdom and today she lives in Illinois with her husband Bernard and three children Afia, Kojo and Jojo.

Her favorite quote is "**Success is by CHOICE not by CHANCE**"

For more information about Lovina visit

> http://www.lovinaakowuah.com/
> www.unleashyourgreatnessbook.com

For Coaching visit:
http://www.lovinaakowuah.com/coaching/

For Speaking Engagements visit:

http://www.lovinaakowuah.com/speaking-engagements/

Email: Lovina.Akowuah@gmail.com

Like us on Facebook: "Lovina Akowuah"

References

(1) http://www.mastermindevent.com/blog/2012mlm
     /#sthash.LfICRA67.dpbs (page 19)

(2) (http://homebusiness.about.com/b/2012/04/13/
     mlm-success-rate-statistics.htm) or (http://mlm-
     thetruth.com/research/mlm-statistics/shocking-
     stats/)

(3) What makes a good mentor: Dr. John V.
     Richardson Jr., Associate Dean, UCLA Graduate
     Division, August 2005

The Business Of The 21st Century- Robert Kiyosaki 1994

Building Your Network Marketing Business Audio CD -
Jim Rohn , 2000

Compound Effect (Multiplying your success~ One simple
step at a time) – Darren Hardy, 2010

Bonus

Write down your daily to do list for the next 21 days. This will keep you focused, organized and help you to be consistent in attaining your goal. The rationale behind this is that most habits are created in 21 days of practice and repetition!

DAY 1

To do List

Starting the Journey is exciting and easy ~ Lovina B Akowuah

If you want accountability send this list to your mentor

DAY 2

To do List

_____

_____

_____

_____

_____

_____

_____

_____

_____

DAY 3

To do List

_____

_____

_____

_____

_____

_____

_____

_____

_____

DAY 4

To do List

DAY 5

To do List

DAY 6

To do List

_____

_____

_____

_____

_____

_____

_____

_____

DAY 7

To do List

_____

_____

_____

_____

_____

_____

_____

_____

_____

DAY 8

To do List

_____

_____

_____

_____

_____

_____

_____

_____

_____

_____

DAY 9

To do List

DAY 10

To do List

_____

_____

_____

_____

_____

_____

_____

_____

_____

DAY 11

To do List

DAY 12

To do List

DAY 13

To do List

DAY 14

To do List

DAY 13

To do List

DAY 14

To do List

DAY 15

To do List

DAY 16

To do List

_____

_____

_____

_____

_____

_____

_____

_____

DAY 17

To do List

DAY 18

To do List

DAY 19

To do List

DAY 20

To do List

DAY 21

To do List

Congratulations, you are well on your way to achieving greatness in your life.

Prayer

<u>Lord, Bless Me in the work I do</u>

Lord, I pray you would show me what work I am supposed to be doing. If it is something other than what I am doing now, reveal it to me. If it is something I am to do in addition to what I am already doing, show me that too. Whatever it is you have called me to do, both now and in the future, I pray you will give me the strength and energy to get it done well. May i find great fulfillment and satisfaction in every aspect of it, even the most difficult and unpleasant parts. Thank you that in all labor there is profit of one kind or another (Proverbs 14:23) ~ **Stormie Omartian (A book of prayer)**

www.ingramcontent.com/pod-product-compliance
Lightning Source LLC
LaVergne TN
LVHW051057080426
835508LV00019B/1921